I dedicate this book to anyone grieving,
You are never alone.

Deeper Than the Ocean is a gift to the reader. A powerful story told in both poetic and narrative form, it pulls the reader through Emma's love, loss, and pain. It is raw, and it hurts to read. But we are drawn to read on. Emma shows us how she uses writing to give voice to her pain—to let the words come out because they must. Writing is Emma's way of dealing with the loss of her close friend, her soulmate.

When Gus died, we all died too. The people we were, people who lived in a world with Gus alive, shriveled up and blew away. Now we lived in a world in which Gus had died, suddenly and wrongly. We were all left in shock, and we didn't know what to do with our pain. Emma gave voice to her pain. I realized this when I first read her gift to us, and I wept. Emma found a way to express her grief and pain—not to *get over it*, but to live on with it. So many of us must live with the loss of a loved one—and more often, with the loss of a person who died young, or unexpectedly.   We must be allowed to feel our pain, and supported while we find ways to live with it—no matter what caused it.

Emma **managed** to live in and with her pain when she wrote this brave work. And as I thought more about it, I realized that Gus was doing it too, when he wrote.

I see even more why Emma and Gus are soulmates. Their souls, their persons, compelled them to express their pain by writing it. In her book, It's OK That You're Not OK, Megan Devine writes "Death doesn't end a relationship. It changes it." I am still Gus's mother. Oskar and Gus are still brothers. Emma is still Gus's soulmate, and we can see that in her book.

To read Deeper Than the Ocean is to be pulled through their friendship and Emma's quest to give the pain of her loss its own voice. I am glad she gave this to us.

Liza K. Womack
Huntington, NY
29 August 2019

INTRODUCTION

It's hard to put a start date on it, or even explain the beginning, but i'll try. Our paths merged at a very young age. Third grade to be exact. And to tell you the truth it really seemed like we were destined to meet even earlier than that. He was born in Allentown, PA, I was born in Long Beach, NY. A small, woodsy town no where near the beach and a little town right on the beach just 40 minutes away from NYC. Two totaly different places. At the age of 5 I had to leave Long Beach behind for a couple of years. At the time my sister was training for the 2004 Olympics for gymnastics. She left about a year before us to train 6-8 hours a day at a very intense gym pretty far away from our Long Beach home. Bouncing around living with different teammates for quite a while at the young age of 13, my mom decided it would be best to move us all out there... And you wouldn't believe where the gym was, Allentown, PA. And the weirdest part... at around the same time Gus ended up moving to our little beach town.

My dad had stayed back in Long beach those two years. Which is where we ended back at after tragically an injury ended my sisters olympic dreams at no place other than the olympic trials. Fast forward to third grade. We end up in the same elementary school, which probably doesn't seem too weird but considering we lived on opposite ends of town and there was about 5 different elementary schools between us, it really was quite weird. He used to tell me he remembered the first day I walked into school. "With your bright blonde hair and goofy smile" Which I still don't know if I believe because I don't personally remember much of third grade besides our teacher Mrs. Camacho and dreading to go to school for the very first time after my dads friend had died the night before, right on the boulevard where our house stood that I just so happened to drive by and see.

My first experience of death: Life changing.

It still shocks my family how much that affected me. I even went to a medium once and my dads friend came through and said how surprised he was that it affected me that much. But there I was in school the next day, my mom wrote the teacher a letter explaining what happened and I got to sit in the "special bean bag chair" all day. No one seemed to pay much attention to me that day or at least my 3rd grade self thought. But Gus did. He would not stop coming over to me that day. Doing any silly thing just to make me laugh. The one person to put a smile on my face. The first of many times he was able to shine some light on a dark day.

We happened to be in every class together for the rest of elementary school. 5th grade was the first year he asked me to be his girlfriend. My first boyfriend. And then that summer past and the teenage angst and emotions started to roll in. And not to mention the awkward growth spurts. You know the ones where the girls grow a foot taller than the boys and there new perky boobs are about the same height as the boys heads. Yea, thats what happened to me. I've been about 5'7 since 7th or 8th grade. And that's about the time all the "older boys" started to show some interest in me. Gus absolutely hated it. We'd be friends for a week then date for two and then we'd hate each other for three and that's just basically how it went for the rest of grade school. Senior year it started to change. We started to grow up some more, showed a little PDA for once, started to sleep at each other's houses, well not exactly started too because that definitely happened before senior year but actually started to wake up next to each other in the morning. Because before that someone was always sneaking out in the middle of the night, and by someone I mean him, which drove me absolutly crazy! (The fights after that definitely lasted a little bit longer than 3 weeks) And all without our parents knowing of coarse.

After high school we both just so happened to have a plan of moving to California. He would move to Los Angeles with Brennan and I moved to San

Diego with my sister to take care of her newborn. I think I was there maybe 3 weeks before I went up to visit him. Everything changed after that. We were serious for once. My first real relationship. My first love. We'd been saying 'I love you' for years at that point but we actually began to realize what it really meant. All we had was each other. That year was strange for the both of us. I gained about 20 lbs, you know the freshman 15 except I wasn't in college, just eating as much as my pregnant sister. Gus dropped about 10, he looked like a skeleton, the skinniest anybody had ever seen him. He had no money at all and no job. He lived on the canned beans his mother would send in a box from New York. Sometimes i'd even steal a bag of groceries from my sister for him to bring when I went up there. We were both lost, tring to find our direction and the closest thing to home was each other. I went to see him almost every other week. I was making about $100 a week and i'd spend about $75 just on the train ride. That lasted about 6 months and then he called me and told he was moving back to New York... tomorrow. I was so upset. He was my everything here, what was I supposed to do without him? I had work in the morning, 6 am. But I was not going to let anything hold me back from seeing him one last time. It was about around 8pm when he told me. And as soon as my sister fell asleep I stole her car and took it 2 and a half hours away to him in LA. We packed his things up, cuddled and cried most of the night. I took him to the airport and kissed him goodbye not knowing the next time I'd see him. And without realizing this would be the first of many times I'd have to do that.

I drove myself home heartbroken just before 7am. My sister caught me but I didn't even care at that point. I wanted to be fired or something I wanted just about any excuse to move back home with him. I stuck it out for about a week and then I couldn't take it anymore, I told my sister I quit and I moved back home about a month after him.

That's when he really started to go hard with the music, and his anxiety was going even harder. His tattoo collection grew fast and I swear the more he got the less he'd show himself in public. In our judgemental small town you couldnt really blame him. He was destined for something bigger then that town, especially looking like that. We basically locked ourselves in his small room of his moms house for a whole year.

And then the music started blowing up, I mean really blowing up. He was always making music, always busy, his followers were growing, all these known people were calling him and the plans he was making just kept growing and growing... and I didn't seem to be apart of any of them. I wish I could explain how that felt but I think that would be a whole book in itself. I'll put it this way, as much as I wanted to be happy for him I couldn't help but feel hurt and betrayed. It hurt like hell. I drove myself crazy. How could he leave me? Am I not good enough for him now? He promised we'd always be together. I was just so scared. I grew so attached to him, it felt like I physically needed him just to breathe and I knew he was going to have to leave me behind, at least for the time being. But he always promised me he'd come back for me. I really believed it too.

But like I said, our start is pretty hard to remember but that day he never came back, that's something i'll never forget.

No matter how hard I try too.

He was here for a long time (practically my whole life)
and then he was gone, and then here again, then gone
again, he went back and forth,
A lot.
Until the day he actually left, and then the day he *really*
left after that.
The whole relationship was back and forth,
upside down,
completely backwards sometimes.

But the love never died,
even after he did.

We were never very good at moving on,
I don't think I ever will.

To write something down is to remember. To contain a memory. It's no longer just wandering in an endless dark abyss with everything else that ponders my thoughts.

Well here I am.

I've never been very good at expressing myself. I have conversations in my head and they sound fine to me but once I go to write them down I can never make much sense of it all. My thoughts are constantly rambled into one giant black hole that escape down the pit of my memory the second I go to open my mouth. I've always struggled sharing anything too deep about myself. Vulnerability overwhelms me. I like to have my secrets, they make me feel safe and in control of myself. I like the mask I wear in front of others. It lets me choose who I am, and what you think of me. To open up to someone is to put trust in them. To take off the mask is to truly find comfort in them. Oh, the amount of thoughts i've had stolen from me. I have put my trust and secrets into people who have completely taken them from me. Isn't that strange? You can share everything with someone and then suddenly they're gone... It's like everything you have ever told them, every cryptic, dark, deep secret is trapped in a box that has been thrown over seas, swirling into the blackness of the mysterious, endlessly deep ocean with nothing, not even a key to help you open it- if only you were ever lucky enough to find it again. They're all just gone. Slipped through your fingers. You are no longer in control of them. I can remember always thinking this way about my "secrets". Ever since I was a little girl, I always knew to be careful of who I told certain things to or what I chose to tell. If I tell them what I know I wouldn't mind to be locked in their minds forever then it won't ever really trouble me. If it's something that I know will eventually eat at my brain knowing someone else had access too it then it escapes my mind so damn quickly I could never even remember I wanted to share the thought with another being.

But If I CHOOSE to share as
many of my thoughts on here as
I can, then whos in control?

He wrote, so I wrote.
It wasn't til we were pretty deep in our mess that I
started too.
It helped and it hurt, and sometimes I think it maybe
made the pain even harder.

More real,
Harder to ignore.

"Pre Evolution, Post Execution"

A series of poems I've had lying around the notes of my phone. There was a lot of shit bottled up in my chaotic mind for a long time and the only way I could escape it was by writing about it. Some didn't seem to make sense, while others were so intensified I still get flashbacks of the anger, depression, and confusion I was feeling the moment I wrote them. I like to think that I've found some clarity in this mess so to take me back to that time is very unnerving. The feelings surface up but I still somehow manage to push them back down again.

SELF DESTRUCT

Baby it makes me sick the way that I love you.
It makes me sick to my stomach now when I hear your name,
And it sounds even worse when I hear it out of someone else's mouth,
Jealousy,

Hold my hair back.
You make me feel nauseous,
Sick to my stomach,
Why the hell do I love you?

Fucked in the head,
Driving down the highway,
Hazy,
I wanna crash so you miss me,
How disgusting is that?
Losing my worth,
Losing my soul,
You've got it in your hands,
Clenching in your fist,
Let me go,
Let me go!

I wanna leave you alone,
It's what you deserve,
The Devils words,
They cut so deep,
When I hear them tremble off your tongue,
Tell me you love me I need to hear it again,
Even if you don't just try to pretend,

How did we get here?
Where did we go?
When did you leave me,
Here all alone?
Left me to rot,
Now I'm dying, all alone,
Rotting on the side of the road.

Addiction

You said you'd be right back,
But where are you?
The winters getting colder,
Living here without you,
The nights are getting longer,
Now that I'm without you,

I'm still exactly where you left me,
Still on the same stuff you gave me,
Can you fight addiction with addiction?
Self conflicting,
Identity crisis,

Can't seem to figure out who I was before you appeared,
Can't seem to find the girl I was the moment you left,
Nothing but false perceptions of each other,
False perceptions of myself,
Who I thought you were is nothing you could be,
Who I thought I was has burned from the fire you started,
With nothing left but ash and debri,
Now I've become just a ghost,
False perception of reality.

He left and then so did I,
we were all over the place.
I thought if I just got away i'd be able to save
myself.

I was wrong,
nothing helped.

Execution

Send my body to heaven,
Burn my thoughts to the ground,
Don't want to have to think when he's not around,
He is gone,
Without a trace or a call,
I've wandered the horizon in search for your soul,
Now I find myself lost at sea,
With no help from you,
I started drowning but you didn't even look,
Now I'm 6 feet under,
And all I got is you on my mind.
The memories weigh me so heavy,
I've anchored myself where the ocean ground lies.

Resurrection

Completely alone in a random place,
Convincing myself that I feel safe.
Was needing you just an illusion?

Maybe I'll be good on my own,
Won't have to call you anymore,
Just to ask if everything's okay,
If you're still thinking about me the way I think about you,
If at night when you can't sleep
are you wishing I was still the one beneath your sheets?

Maybe I'll be good on my own,
Maybe there's someone else by now,
Have you moved on?
I don't know why it's so hard to be this strong.

Maybe I'll be good on my own,
Can't find sadness in dying,
Can't find happiness in living,
And the only thing that would make it go away
 would be you standing in front of me telling me it was okay,

But I'm not talking about this you,
I mean the old you,
The one who used to understand what it's like to be someone real,
To feel all the things there is to feel,
The one who could remember what it's like to want to hurt yourself so bad,
You get stuck in a trans like there's no way you'll ever get out,

Do you remember those days?
Are you so far past them that they faded away,
Are they gone forever,
Are you gone forever,
Have I lost my baby?

Spiraling down a never ending abyss,
You,ll never fathom the taste of it,
Taste of who you were before you became who you are.
The sweetest taste I ever got to fathom.

Star shopping?
Baby you **are** the stars in the sky,
How could I buy them?
I just hope you remember that,
before they dim your light black,

Maybe I'll be good on my own,
will you?

What I thought could be the end was just the
beginning of a whole new world with him.
One I couldn't have ever imagined.
He loved me,
I swear he did,
just his actions didn't always seem to follow.
He was lost,
all that running,

**Running from something I never got the
chance to save him from.**

I want to tell you about my love but I can't call him that anymore. I want to tell you how he's managed to escape further and further, day by day, to the back of my mind. To the soft dark oblivion of my memories. When only a couple of months ago he was so far lodged down my throat the only thing I could taste was his name. And every time I spoke, I spoke of it. I spoke of him. He used to pop up with every thought my mind created but now he has slowly dissolved.
Love?
How can I call this love when I can watch it disintegrate in front of my eyes so quickly. I feel you escaping my grasp like a massive handful of sand slipping through the cracks of my fingers one painful sharp grain at a time. But it's going so much faster than I could have ever expected. I could try to speak to you, I just don't know what I would say. The words are tangled up inside my head. You've tried to reach in to brush them through but you just can't seem to find them, you can't even seem to find my hand. I think you're too faraway. Too faraway to grasp it. Our love will soon vanish.
Then I receive your messages that now don't seem like you, I get so addled I can't manage to put all of my thoughts in one little message to send back to you. They slip out of my mind and into the stars one thought at a time, and I can never get them back again.
Maybe I am the one giving up this time.
There is clarity in forgetting but only when the memory is fully consumed. The little pieces you can't seem to swallow into your disappearing thoughts become little nightmares that terrorize your head.
I used to think of you when I was scared.
You were the man of my dreams but I've become an insomniac.
I thought we could manage the distance. But I think you,ve forgotten about me to. Maybe that's what makes this so effortless for me. Child's play. You don't love me like you did when we were kids. Do you remember that? The days when nothing made sense but everything made sense all at the same time. We didn't know the meaning to it all, we didn't even care, all we knew was that we were happy.

One time we were happy.
Clarity in ignorance,
Bliss in the innocence,
What I would do to find that again.

Your words turned to whispers and then into nothing,
Nothing.
You left me with nothing for one month. This may not
seem long to you but to me it seemed like a lifetime.
I was nine years old when we met, I had never gone that
long without you.

And there you were, the second I stepped off the plane,
there you were.
I had dreams of that,
never thought they'd come true.

I still dream of this

Circular Illusions

My life starts to seem like it's spinning in complete circles,
Maybe I've gone mad, maybe I haven't,
Contradictions,
I tell myself one thing and end up doing the complete opposite,
I tell myself I don't want something and yet it becomes the only thing I
desire,
I promise myself I don't need him until I remember the sweet taste of
his lips,
and he becomes the only thing that I crave,
Craving so deeply as I watch him become my mania,
My obsession,
The only thing I could never let go of,
The moment I saw him again my progress of forgetting just burst into
flames,
right in front of my cloudy, water-filled eyes,
How could I be so blinded by his charm,
So genuinely affected by his sweet yet not so innocent smile,
He jabbed his fist through my bony chest,
And once again had his grip so tightly on my heart,
If he dared to move an inch it would tear right out of my chest and kill
me,
Instantly,
And just like that I find myself stuck in the same place I had just finally
escaped.
Did I ever even leave to begin with ?
Maybe it was all in my head.

Suicide

I have fallen yet again into the deep, rigid ditch you dug for me to lay in.
Buried alive with my only chance to survive is to dig my way out.
My fingernails still broken and my hands still blistered from the last time.
How could I of let you do this to me again?
How was it so easy to believe your lies?
They say if you talk to the devil enough times he can convince you to do just about anything.
Maybe that's just what this was.
Your energy constantly brings me down and yet I can't find myself attracted to anything else.
It's like a magnetic force pulling me so deeply, so quickly back into your relentless grip.
If there is one thing I know, oh how I fucking know, is how toxic you are for my damn soul.
But why do I keep finding myself drinking from your poison?
My ignorance vanished long ago when I realized it will soon kill me, replace my innocent blood with your deadly venom.
Until I could no longer breath and I suffocate in your evil ways that you call love...
And yet I find myself everyday wanting to take just one more little sip.

And just like that he was gone... again. I let him
back in and he slipped right through the cracks. I
couldn't blame it on him, not this time.
It was just life getting in the way of us.
Which it just so happened to do,
A LOT.

LET ME LIVE IN A TIME YOU DIDN'T EXIST

They say it takes 11 weeks to get over someone. No contact, no social media, no pictures. I can believe that. On the contrary I think it's takes a whole lifetime to forget a person. If only a lifetime. When the same thing that once made   you happy is now the only thing making you anything but, you tend to want to forget.

To have a wish come true; to wish I never met you wouldn't be a regret. It would've made my life a whole lot easier. But how fun is an easy life anyways? We are all traveling on this journey we call life to learn and experience it through our *own* experiences, so without a little mistake upon each journey how could we ever reach nirvana? Everyday is a new lesson. Every mistake is a lesson. A blessing in disguise. I would like to think of you as more than just a mistake but you make that pretty hard to do. Like the way your face would light up when the lies you spoke of would start rolling of your tongue as I glared right into your motionless eye. You made it so hard for me to question you. Or when you told me you loved me and looked right through my gleaming soul, you made it so easy to trust you. But after you've caused me all of this pain how do I think of you as anything more than just a mistake?

STUCK

Where do you go when you have no motivation to move?
You start to become so content with yourself,
You can stay in one place forever feeding off your own thoughts,
When people's voice start to shake your own voice,
When strangers always stay strange,
You refuse to put the effort out in the universe in order to
connect with a different soul,
I am still learning to connect with my own,
I have been torn in two for so long I now need to know what it's
like to feel whole again,
What it's like to have myself all to myself,
Sometimes it gets scary, and sometime it's feels way to fine,
I feel so ok I can be by myself forever,
I don't want company,
The people start to scare me,
Talking to someone other than myself becomes hard,
I think I can easily drive myself mad,
or is that just how I've inturpertated sanity my whole life?

He was a raging fire in my world, one that would ignite me as well. When we burned together we were huge, strong, and untouchable but when he burned alone he was reckless but beautiful, dissociated but alluring. He scared me. The thought of him alone terrified me. But I knew one day i'd need to leave, i'd have to just give up. But everytime he tried to go I couldn't help but hold on a little longer. My hands blistered and burned, it was painful even standing next to him. Someone I once grew with, watch grow into this massive fire we ignited together... without me. He was so much bigger then me now. And the worst part? He seemed happy.

The smoke he left was dark and cloudy.

Until the day it started to settle.

I tried so hard to let myself heal. Opening myself to new people. Most of them not important enough to even mention.

Except for one.

My new beginning.

Stupid, Meaningless Words

I never knew if I should kiss you or hug you.
I was so used to saying "I love you",
Do I show you I care?
You confuse me with your words you speak so loud,
As you scream the opposite words,
Not only from your mouth.
Your eyes tell me a different story,
Your actions sometimes follow your words,
Sometimes they don't,
You're afraid.
But your mask is falling off,
It's sliding off so slowly,
Now hanging only by the grip of the stubble on your face.
Sometimes I wish I was better with my own words,
So I can tell you it's okay to let it drop,
Shatter too the ground
Too many pieces to clean up.
But every time I try these other words seem to fall out of my own mouth,
Stupid, meaningless words.

But being so codependent for so long I fell right

back into that. I just started to fill the hole in

my heart.

Distract Me

I let you distract me from him,
Time goes by and he becomes a distant memory,
His name fades like the sun light,
Except it never comes back,
Vanished,
But now you've become the moonlight,
Without him, I need you,
 Now I let him distract me from you.

And In the midst of this new beginning he'd still creep in and out. And everytime I saw him I couldn't help myself. Even when I thought i was finally letting go he was able to suck me right back.
As easy as you could have imagined.
And it always hurt like hell waking up realizing he wasn't mine anymore.

Again

I let you tell me you love me,
again
Just because I like the way it bounces off your tongue and into the holes
of my body,
I won't be letting anything but your words inside me.
And then you say it again,
And again,
And just one more time until you convince me.
Your words start to become my memories,
Memories of when those words were true,
Memories that I thought I burned into pieces so many moons ago.
Every nerve shrieking,
Telling me to run,
Every shaking bone in my body telling me to stay.
My mind disappears and now my body's in control,
How did you find yourself this deep?
How did I let you get this far,
again.
And as I let you get deeper and deeper my mind diminishes,
You got what you want.
The word love never slips from your tongue again,
And now,
again,
we sit in a room filled with words I never got to say.

JUST COME BACK TO ME

I think this is the bitter confusion of the whole relationship,
Surfacing all at once,
A glimpse that it might be gone,
And the taste that it could come back,

                                    The delusion that your ok without it,
                                     The fantasy of it walking right back

I quickly felt that hole I was trying to fill hollowing again. I just couldn't get myself to actually connect with anyone. I was grieving from this heartbreak, I was so afraid to let go. I thought maybe he'd just come back, I mean thats whats he had told me. I had to realize maybe we were too far past that. I thought that could be the worst thing i'd ever have to face.

Id realize soon enough it wasn't even close.

But in those moments my hope had disappeared I thought I was too broken to fix, far beyond repair.

PYROMANIA

I can still feel you when he's not around,
I can feel you when he's there,
I've built a temporary home in so many men's arms,
Just to watch the walls burst into flames.
You are the burning match,
And the thought of you, the gasoline.
The fires sway tempts me to join in.
Maybe one day I'll be courageous enough to engulf myself in the smoke,
To swallow the fire, and let it spit out of the pores of my skin,
Screaming.
And end this everlasting pain.

YOU TOLD ME YOU'D NEVER LEAVE

I told myself I wouldn't write about him any longer,
I told myself these poems were hurting me,
Not healing,
Stopping me from letting go,
He seems happy now in his own world that I have no part of,
 I want him to be happy,
 I want to be happy again too, so badly,
But every time I thought I was doing better,
He'd leave me a message,
 Sometimes even letters,
He'd say I still love you.
I just want you to know,
When i'm done with this all,
We can go all the places you ever wanted to go,
We'll get married,
Own a castle of our own,
I was taunted by this idea,
That he would never actually
leave me alone,
And then i'd see him,
I never quite knew what to
expect,
Sometimes he was the person I
knew,
And sometimes he was the person
i'd regret,
All those dreamy words he had
said,
I'd be better off to just forget.

It was hard to remind myself it was over when I was being told it may not be. It was even harder to listen to his words when he was showing me the complete opposite.

SOMETHING YOU NEED TO REMEMBER

If its so easy for him to say goodbye,
Remember there is something,
On the other side,
He seems to want more.

I was angry, jealous, and still so dissapointed but in the middle of all of this heartbreak and confusion there was a relief, my *new beginning* had never given up, even when I had. He was consistent, knew what he wanted. And he was actually helping me feel better. He was making me feel important again. He made me feel like life might be worth it. That feeling was overwhelming.
Sometimes I felt like I was even betraying him but, how could I be?
He seemed to have already moved on himself. And to make matters worse it seemed like he was just shoving it in my face at that point.
But I still denied my new love for a long time, Until the day I couldn't anymore.

These feelings surfaced up all at once and just like that it felt like maybe just maybe I was healing. I was actually happy for the first time in a LONG time. But I was scared.
How can I just let this happen again?
And he was so sweet, how could I just drag him into this mess of mine?

The mess we had no idea had only just started.

A STUPID FLY, DIES IN YET ANOTHER WEB

Lust,
What a fucking ridiculous emotion,
and one I feel far too much,
A somewhat sweet catastrophe.
The acceptance of a heart break,
whether it be yours or his,
The fasaude that you just may be falling,
The questioning of your mental stability for letting yourself feel
this deep,
yet so shallow over a complete stranger,
The pathetic realization that you have somehow found yourself
all wrapped up

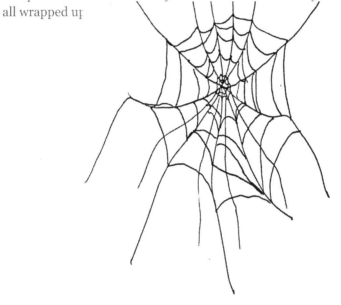

LUCIFERS RECRUITER

Watch as I tear the spell you cast upon me
right out of my own aura,
The second you think you have me is the
second I disappear.
You lack emotion and I learn from every
moment.
Show me your true colors and I'll show you
the contrast of mine.
The moment I feel is the moment I run.
Comfort will never satisfy me.
I will bite your bait so hard you would bet your life I'd be there
when you reeled me up.
But just to see your satisfaction crumble is what I yearn for most.
If you could tamper with my emotions let me show you how hard
I can play with yours.
How fucked up could I be to wanna hurt something that doesn't
wanna hurt me.
You're so naive.
I'm sorry I've sucked you in so deep,
Just to spit you right out.
You almost thought I enjoyed the taste of you,
But not enough to let it turn bitter,
Just a little sample so you can always stay sweet.
Spit you right back to earth before the gods realize you weren't
the angel I need,
You're just far too kind to lay beside someone like me.

FEARING THE LET GO

Show me you love me with your hands tied around my neck,
Spit out your feelings as you spit in my mouth.
Grip me tighter in fear of me letting go,
Deeper and deeper into this shallow hole
Love me now but never tell a soul,
Love me now until it gets old.
The fear of my own self turning cold.

Something I'll never be able to explain to you;

He is starting to scare the shit out of me as I think of how you destroyed me. You'll always ignite this fear in me. He's starting to stare into me eyes the way you once did, the way you looked at me in a crowded room like I was the only girl there. And then I remember how quickly you stopped looking at me like that, how quickly the other girls stole your glare and that makes me want to run, run fast for the hills. But for some reason my feet are stuck. It feels like there's stones in my shoes. I'm so afraid but I can't get myself to leave. I'm starting to enjoy his company, but I know exactly what comes next... it starts off like this: It's like I have all the security in the world until I find someone who can reinsure it for me and they disappear and so does my security of myself. I'm stuck, i'm stuck even further behind the starting point, I don't have nearly the amount of confidence I had before you came along. All of it is gone, I have to start all over again and it's scary, it's fucking scary to be somewhere with yourself where you don't even know who you are, where you don't even want to be who you are. And then everybody's gone because knowing me I'll push everyone away when I find someone to love me, I start to think they're all I need. Just the feeling of someone needing me; until they leave and I realize how much I fucking needed them, I needed them so much more than they ever needed me, so much that I am not whole without them. You'll break me. I put so much into another being I lose myself, pieces of myself are stolen.... actually I won't even say stolen, nobody forced me to give you these pieces, I myself sacrifice myself but for what reason? There is no reason. For love? For lust? That's just pathetic. Oh, but don't have pity on me because I do it to myself, right? How hard I let myself fall, how high up I'll let myself drop just to shatter, and that's why I can't. I feel it happening already and I wanna run, I wanna run so far away from you. Every time you leave my side I convince myself how much I don't like you even though I know that's not true. But I need too I can't do this to myself again the pain is still there from the last time and it still fucking hurts. Maybe you won't be the one to hurt me? Right? That's what I'd like to believe too but the chances are you will. And what if you do bring that pain back? I can't have that, I just can't handle it. I can handle a lot of shit but not my own security crumbling in my own two hands, because of my own fatal grip. Everything I just got back to just escape my grasp and it'll happen so quickly I probably wouldn't even notice fast enough to pick the broken pieces of myself back up.

It's my own self righteousness getting the best of me if I don't leave. It's like I'm pushing a self destruct button. The worst part is that I never deserved this, it just happens; someone comes around and fucks up every meaning of love you ever created in your mind and replaces it with resentment. What's even worse than that, is how much you don't deserve that... And I know that if you're not going to be the one to hurt me i'll be the one hurting you.

A lot could happen in one summer, and it did.
We were falling in love,
I was feeling something again,
Something intense.
I really didn't think I was capable of falling in love with someone else, but it was inevitable.
There was something there I could no longer fight anymore.

REAL nauseating FEELS

If you asked me what I thought of love a year ago I would have thought of
something a little among the lines of this, I would have told you that love is an
extremely intense emotion, and I would've almost subconsciously paired the
word intense to something negative. I craved the negativity I craved the toxicity
of a relationship, I craved the jealousy, I craved the dramatic reactions. Maybe it
was my immaturity, maybe it was the men I was falling for, maybe I just didn't
know any better. And then you came around and kept coming around until I had
you. And now I do, I have all of you but it's not fake this time. I feel it, I feel you
when you're not around. I can feel you feeling for me. You make me endure
something I never knew I ever even craved. Something I never knew I wanted. I
feel passion in the way that you kiss me. When you touch your soft lips against
my senseless ones I can actually feel something. I feel your warmth, I can feel
your purity. When you touch me I just want to grab you ten times harder against
me because it feels almost electric to have your body rubbing against mine. And
then you look me in the eyes and I could cry, I could cry just writing about it. You
make me feel loved, you make me feel accepted, but better then that you make me
feel more than that. You make me feel more of myself. Without even any words.
Your silence isn't empty. And I've never heard something scream so loud that I
couldn't physically hear at all.. until now, until you.

You scare me and make me feel so safe all at one time. There's no more pain
associated with the word love, there's fear but no pain. But the fear stems from
my own insecurities from my past relationships, the fear stems from losing you.
It's not fear of you. You nearly do the opposite. You make me feel undamaged,
unbroken like no one ever hurt me. For the moments I lie in your arms I feel just
as beautiful and whole as you. I can feel myself healing.
I don't think I've ever felt the love I was supposed to feel, the love I should've
been given. I've felt love from comfort, I've felt love from jealousy, I've felt love
from feeling protected, and I've felt love from pain and sorrow and vulnerability
but never just from something so raw, from something so sweet. So sweet it feels
like it could never go sour. And the angst of you not feeling the same is
nonexistent. Because I can feel it in your eyes, I can feel it in your presence that
you feel the same.

I always feared a love like this because I thought it'd be boring and unfulfilling. I
always thought you needed some kind of darkness to *feel* at all which is so
morally fucked up, but at the same time true it's just what I thought. But this
doesn't feel that way. It doesn't feel like that. It's stimulating, it's overwhelming,
it's exciting and it's sweet and it's tender and most of all it's *real* and it's as
beautiful as you are, and just as you make me feel.

Oh I was happy,
We were happy,
We really were.
And I was ready, so ready to take that chance
again.
I completely forgot how good the beginning is,
The relationship with no baggage of its own.
I never thought i'd be able to let go like this.
I was finally starting to heal.

THE CONTOTINIST

I dangled from the clouds, wrapped in the frail ribbons
of your love,
I watched the threads that made up the fabric holding
my life rip one after the other.
Burning the layers of my skin as I slid so delicately
against it,
Until I finally fell from the sky expecting you to catch
me.
Your arms disappeared as quickly as the ground
smacked up from under me.
You left me raw, skinned to death,
lying on the cold concrete.
My flesh bleeding out, guts sticking to cement,
Emotions ripped right out of me, the pain lingered
along with it.
Waves of the duo would come in and out.
The agony would come in slowly,
Creeping into the blood in my veins,
to the guts of my stomach,
A wretched agony.
Then it would come out faster than the blink of an eye,
A quick taste of freedom,
Til the moment it would come inching right back.

The thought of this going away was just a mere facade,
And then in my illusions someone came along.
The out would last much longer,
It was a full plate of freedom now.

Until he'd leave,
The tiniest memory would creep its way back into my
brain,
Like cancer; it spread so quickly,
I thought I'd never be cured.
But the small doses of him started to become large
doses,
and I could swear his medicine was working.
You no longer poisoned my brain,
He did.
But it wasn't poison,
Not nearly as deadly.
It was an antidote,
But it was as pure as can be,
A cure.
Wounds I never thought could heal,
Starts healing right in front of my eyes.
Scars I never thought would fade,
Have completely disappeared.
Memories I thought would distort my brain forever,
 have been completely repossessed.
I've untangled myself from you,
I am free from your contortion,
And I have willingly wrapped myself around his finger,
Just to contort myself again.

November 15th

The worst day of my life, November 16th 5:30 am.
My sister called me that night at a strange time, I told myself if she were to call again id pick up. I had work in the morning so I wanted to get to sleep early. She didn't call, so I fell asleep. I woke up that morning to the sound of my moms voice gently saying my name but her tone was off, it was too gentle...I knew there was something wrong.
"What's wrong mom? What's wrong?!"
"I don't know how to tell you this Emma"
There was a long pause, I realized my dad should be home. I thought she would tell me something had happened to him fighting a fire, I thought I knew what was about to come out of her mouth, and then she said it.
I was so wrong.
"Gus died"
And then there were the screams, the strange body movements. I cried so much that day I broke a blood vessel under my eye.
There was no comfort in denying, there was no 'let me check to see if this is real'. I knew my mom wouldn't tell me something like that without knowing.
I just somehow knew it was real.
I dont think ill ever be able to make the sounds that came out of my mouth that day.
That pain haunts me.
I think of those words all the time.
"Gus died",
those horrible fucking words.

THAT AWFUL MORNING

I got one missed call,
Before I went to bed,
My sister,
That was all,
I told myself if she called again,
I'd roll up out of bed and answer,
She never did call back,
So I fell back asleep,
I woke to my mother,
At my door,

5am,
Tears in her eyes,
She told me you had died,
I screamed in my bed,
For what seemed like days,

Only 6am,
They told me not too, but I did,
I called your mama,
With all the same screams;
"No not him, why'd it have to to be him?"
He was the only one I needed,
She told me "honey I'm sorry",
I didn't have much left to say,
When the rest of our lives seemed so grey,

7am,
I called my friend,
So many times I thought I'd break the line,
I waited in bed for someone to call back,
For what seemed like a lifetime,

It was only 8am,
I screamed in my bed,
Holding my own hand,
Staring at a picture of you,
Your voice singing in my ear,
A song I hadn't listened too,
since the day you left me in your room,
Screaming the words so loud,
I thought I'd stopped breathing,

It was now 9:30am,
My friends tiptoed into my room,
To see a sight they wish they hadn't,
Blood vessels broken apart all over my face,
From the amount of tears I'd been crying,
They told me they were sorry,
But nothing made it better,
The time was moving slower than ever,
I felt cold to the bone,
I wrapped myself in all your clothes,
Even that big ugly sweater,

10 in the morning,
Seemed like it was never ending,
And for about 3 months,
I swear, It didn't.

NOTHING IN THIS WORLD WILL EVER BE THE SAME

How do I ever move on past this pain,
How can I just go through a normal day without thinking of you,
How does the world keep spinning when your heart has stopped beating,
I'll listen for you everywhere I go,
I want everything to stop,
I want to sit here and drown myself in our memories,
I don't know how you ever let this go,
I don't know how I'll ever move forward,
I don't know how to do this without you.

I CAN'T STOP LOOKING FOR YOU

It's like everyday that I wake up,
I wish I was waking up from this
chaos,
It's like everyday is a nightmare that I
just can't seem to escape,
It's like you were just here last week,
but now there's no where to find you,
I shut my eyes and search for you in
my head,
I shut my lights, hoping I'll see you in
the dark,
And when I'm breaking down, I search
for you through my tears,
I will search for you forever,
Through my tears,
Through the dark,
And through this scary place I call my head,
I will feel you.

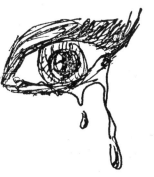

I NEVER THOUGHT OF A KISS SO COLD

I walked into that pale lit room,
Your mama by my side,
My eyes filled with tears,
As I peeled them off the ground,
And onto that box they kept you in,
Where they laid your pretty head,
And not only that but your body too,
You laid there silent,
With all of your screaming tattoos,
Your lips were the same,
Your nose was too,
But it was just your body,
It was empty of you,
I was afraid I'd have flashbacks,
And believe me I do,
But if I never got that last kiss,

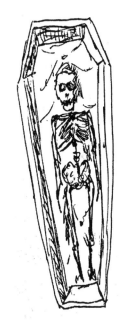

I'd still be waiting here for you.

I DON'T WANT IT TO GET BETTER

Everyday I hear it's going to get better,
But what if I don't want it too?
What if the only time I really feel you,
Is when I'm screaming through my crys?
What if when I smile you disappear thinking
that I'm fine?
I'm scared of being ok,
For some reason I don't really want this pain to
end.

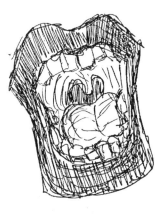

GUILT

I see that you're dying but there's nothing I can do,
I'm miles and miles away from reach of you.
We drifted so far away,
All I can see is our memories,
From the dust and debri.
All I got left is this picture of you and me.
Our love caught on fire set by another us,
You were burned by the smoke.
Somehow I escaped out the rabbit hole,
I didn't mean to,
I slipped,
But I watched you burn right in front me,
With my limbs chained against the floor,
I couldn't help you at all.

SWEET ANGEL

Don't feed these feelings,
I can't take the bleeding.
I'm feeling dizzy,
Light headed,
The world is spinning.
You were far in the distance,
But at least you were there.
Now you're so far.
I can't seem to care,
About the world,
I've came to bare,
Everyday.
Cold stares.
I broke a mirror once,
Is it my fault?
Is it my luck?
I can't help but blame myself,
For all the things I could've helped.
I gave up when you told me too.
I never wanted too,
All I ever wanted was you.
Sweet, sweet angel baby,
Your halo burns my eyes.
I can't stop these cries.

MY CEILING IS TORTURING ME

How can anything make sense again if I'm not looking into your eyes.
I howl at my bedroom ceiling,
just wishing you were still breathing.
I could hear the beating of people's hearts,
And I want to rip them right out of their chest and hand it to you.
I close my eyes and picture you next to me,
But then I force them open and see nothing but this closing in ceiling.
I would trade anything just to have you laying here with me,
I'd do anything even just to say goodbye one last time as you were
leaving.
The corners of my eyes have become raw,
 It hurts more and more every time I cry,
This burning, stinging pain,
It hurts so much but I just can't stop.
These cuts are so deep,
I can't stop the bleeding,
I don't see them ever healing.

I GUESS MY PAINTINGS FINISHED

I miss him,
I miss him when I close my eyes to go to sleep,
I miss him when I open them in the morning,
I miss him when the sun peeks through my bedroom window,
I remember how he'd wake me up if I slept later then him,
I remember that when it seems to hard to open up the blinds and go on.
I remember how he'd cuddle me until his body got too hot,
And he'd peel his warm skin off mine,
He'd turn away from me and start to fall asleep,
For some reason I always needed something,
somewhere on us to be touching when we slept,
Just the subtle touch of his hand would calm me,
We used to fight about who got the inside of the
bed,
I'd tell him he was supposed to get the outside,
he's the guy,
But now I hate the inside,
I feel trapped without him,
 It feels weird to have nothing left but memories
of someone,
It seems like one big picture you've been painting
in your head for so long,
That you got so lost in it you started to forget it
might just be your imagination,
All I have are these little figments ofl the time we
spent together,
These figments are now all I have to paint you
with,
There's nothing left to add.

TOO MANY TOMORROWS WITHOUT YOU

I open my eyes to the walking dead,
The world is dead to me.
The people,
With their blank stares and motionless faces.
How could anyone understand the shit I've been facing?
The pain I have been given.
The weight on my shoulders slowly and painfully pushing me deeper
into the ground,
The roots have gotten wrapped around my ankles,
And they don't seem like they'll ever let go,
Constantly treading on the thought that I won't be engulfed by the dirt
today,
Afraid of the dark settling in,
Into the bones of my body that were never exposed to such filth,
Exposed to the heart that's been too busy keeping me alive,
The heart that I can feel now skipping beats every moment I think of you
The heart I can feel slowing down ever since you've left,
Slowing down with the darkness of the world slipping into my blood,
Blood and sweat being replaced by blackness.
My brain circling in just some faint memories,
Unable to soak in any further information of the world.
Unable to want too.
Unable to go on.

Today turns into to tomorrow,
The weight of the world slamming down on my shoulders,
My feet pressing harder and further into the soil,
The vines start to tangle so tightly around my limbs,
My lungs finally fill with the dirt I've been trying so hard to spit out,
The burning of my eyes,
The tears drying completely out,
My whole body smothered in darkness,
The ending of my last tomorrow.

CLEANING MY NAILS, YET AGAIN

I want to scream on the top of my lungs every time I see a picture of you,
Every time I hear your voice I dig in my brain to remember the sound of
your breathe,
I dig so hard pieces of my brain get stuck underneath my fingernails,
And it's so painful.
I shove it right back in as far back as it could go.
I'm running from the pain,
I'm running so fast but it's still somehow a step ahead of me.
I'm reminded every time I think I've gone further,
It pulls me by the ends of my hair,
And I crumble to the ground.
I melt into the concrete,
With the thought of you drowning my mind.
Until the whole cycle just repeats itself again,
And I'm ripping my hands out of my brain,
With the chunks still stuck underneath my nails from the last time.

I DON'T WANT TO DROWN ANYMORE

At first I wanted to drown myself in memories of you,
I dove into any part of you there was left.
Now I see the water,
And I run so far away from it,
I feel the pain just by looking at it.
The fear of that pain drowning the organs of my body,
I'm scared if I go back to that,
I won't be able to get myself out.

I lost track of time at some point.
I wasn't working, I wasn't really around anyone, there really wasn't much purpose of time.
It seemed to only make things worse, to think about everyday it'd been without him on this Earth, that really hurt.
It made life seem so pointless.
Even now that feeling that all this time has gone by still makes me want to throw up.
So after a while there really wasn't much of a timeline anymore, it was just quite a mess.
I literally couldn't think about anything but him and sometimes that made me just want to forget about it all completely.
My emotions ran wild, the smallest thing ticked me off. I could cry at nearly anything but at the same time nothing really seemed that bad compared to this.
I didn't want to talk unless it was about him.
I didn't want to be around anyone who didn't know him and even those people I couldn't be around for long.
It seemed like everyone was moving on with their life.
And at the time I felt betrayed by that.
How could they?
I just couldn't, I wouldn't let myself.
There was times I really felt crazy.
I scared the shit out of myself.
Diagnosing myself every other day, by the end of every week I'd have about 5 new mental disorders according to WebMD.
Nothing seemed to make sense anymore, especially people.
I couldn't help the hate growing in my body.
There was nothing sweet anymore, it all just seemed so bitter.

Shriveled Up Eyes

I try not to hate the world,
But it's so hard now that you're gone,
I have so much love around me,
But somehow I feel so empty,
Hollow as the casket they put you in,
My smiles been see through,
Just like my heart,
I can tell you "I love you",
But I can't tell you where it started,
Ever since you everything's been disregarded,
Everyone seems so concerned,
but no one seems to actually want to learn,
Learn whats been driving me insane,
To busy with their own day to days,
While I'm here struggling to make it through another night,
Everyday forcing my eyes open to see the light,
The sun burning my eyes,
My eyes that have cried so many tears they're already too dry,
These bloodshot eyes watching the world as it passes me by.

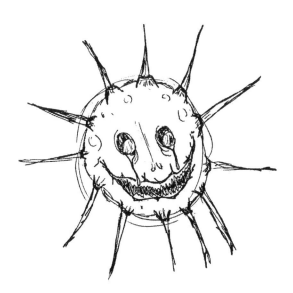

To My Aunt Stephy

I feel a connection to someone I never knew,
She was only 22,
Writing poems in the dark,
With just candle light,
Knocking them over on purpose,
Just to see if she'd burn as quick as this fragile paper,
How quick she'd turn to ashes,
But everyone around her was constantly trying to save her,
Save her from something she didn't know she'd never let herself overcome,
It devoured her in the lonely night,
When the candles weren't shining,
She let her darkness eat away at her until she was starving.
And all I got are they're empty stories half untold,
But somehow even with just that alone,
I feel this link to someone I never knew,
Because somehow I feel just like you.

I'M NOT OKAY

Was loving you a dream?
I swear I have memories,
I didn't just hallucinate.
I swear you were there,
In front of my stare,
But I keep waking up,
And you don't even exist anymore,

Am I in hell?
Because if I had it my way,
You'd be here today,
But I continue to wake up,
Without you in my days.

I swear these are the roses u gave me,
Last Valentine's Day,
I lay here wishing to go back to sleep,
Because I seem to only see you,
In my darkest of dreams,

I'm writing suicide notes,
Just to feel close,
I feel so detached to my body,
Ever since you floated away,
Nothing seems real,

Please help me,
I'm really not okay.

STILL CAN'T SHUT MY EYES

The nights the darkest,
Right when I'm closing my eyes,
The hardest,
The tiredness I feel from faking this smile,
But I still can't shut my eyes.
The lies I repeat,
Exhaust me,
But still can't shut my eyes.
The words you told me,
Haunt me,
I remember your cold closed eyes,
And now I really can't shut mine.
It's half passed three,
I've drained myself empty,
And now finally I fall asleep.
Wake up to birds chirping,
It's 8 in the morning,
Just another day of misery.

LOST HOPE

The ground under me,
The air surrounding me,
I surrender to the thought of you,
The one that's been trying to drown my thoughts all day,
I think of your eyes,
And I sit here and cry,
Screaming your name in vain,
I talk to you in public,
With my headphones in,
Without the music playing,
I never care what people think,
Until I stop,
And I realize what I'm doing;
I'm talking to the wind,
To a boy I once had the chance to lay next to every night,
I'm talking to the wind pretending it's you,
But it's so empty,
There's nothing to touch,
Nothing to hold,
There's not even an answer back,
But I continue to do it,
I don't know why,
I continue to lie,
And tell everyone I feel you by my side,
But really I don't feel anything but this cold wind,
Freezing my cries.

TWO LOST SOULS

It's not easy to forget the agony drowning my head,
I'm slipping underwater,
But the water feels as warm as my blood so it doesn't even matter,
I'm stuck in your undertow,
And I can't find the strength to let go,
My mouth fills with sand,
And the reef smacks up against my brain,
I'm lost in the darkness of the sea,
But now you feel so much closer to me,
The firm grip of someone tryna save me,
The last thing I ever wanted;
To save a life that's been nothing but haunting,
Now I'll have flashbacks of this,
Just like I do of you,
Like of me and you playing chicken in that pool,
Our life was a metaphor,
Constantly saving each other from drowning,
Until you slipped away from my grip,
And I couldn't pull you out of the spiraling downfall,
But now who's gonna be here to pick me up when I try to end it all,
I guess we'll meet wherever it is that's after this,
Or maybe we won't,
Because who would ever give two lost souls,
Everything they ever hoped.

THE PAIN, IT NEVER ENDED

You told me you cared,
But I always questioned it,
How could you love me and leave?
I thought 3,000 miles apart was the furthest we'd ever be,
How naive,
Now we're in different dimensions,
With no communication,
And there's nothing more to see.
My brain was just deceiving me,
I thought we'd have a chance,
But a chance becomes absolute,
When there is nothing,
Not even doubt.

The pain,
It never ended,
And my body never mended,
And nothing you left me with ever ended up fixing me,
Your clothes they kept me warm,
But your cards they left me scorned,
And that mug you gave me dropped and shattered to the floor,
And as I picked the pieces up,
I decided which one would cut,
The deepest incision I could bare,
Just to maybe find you there,
In my slowly motionless glare,

I thought about the stars,
And where we fell apart,
And I dreamt of you,
Sewing my bloody scars shut.
My heart that beat for you,
You tied it like a shoe,
And just when I'm about to wake up,
A kiss by the stroke of luck,

The air,
It hits my lips,
I'm still laying on the floor,
One more day of life,
Am I happy,
I'm unsure,
Am I dancing,
Or at war.

NEEDLES

You told me stay grounded,
But now I just can't move,
These vines that you had watered,
Thorns have started piercing through,
This pain,
I can't escape,

You told me to be happy,
But this smile hurts so bad.
These tears I show only to my pillow,
Oh I feel so alone,

Your sick of seeing me this way,
Well so am I,
Feels like needles in my eye,
But I'm not allowed to cry.

It was hard for me to let love back in.

It was hard for me to just accept it.

Nothing seemed true, everything seemed pointless.

What's was the point?

And I was getting really comfortable spending my
days alone. Less pressure.

But he never gave up on me,

even when I was so close to giving up on myself.

He was there.

But I wasn't, at least not fully.

If I wasn't acting like a complete zombie to
everyone, numb and emotionless.

I was acting completely manic,

mumbling my new theories on death, and my new
self diagnosis. I wasn't much fun to be around,

Probably a bit scary.

And I knew I was hurting him, which just hurt me
even more.

But grief is selfish.

I didn't want to care for anyone but myself.

THEY SAY IT COMES IN WAVES

Grief is strange,
It's selfish.
You can't get yourself to think of anyone else but you,
You don't care about other people problems,
Because who has more problems then you right now?
But you try,
You try everyday to be this better person,
For him, for her, for them,
You're trying,
To make some good out of all of this.
Trying to find that little speck of light,
Amongst the deepest, darkest place you could've ever imagined
yourself in.
The realization that life is too precious to waste,
The realization that *your* heart is still beating,
Even when it feels like it's not.
But then you think of his heart beat,
And just how fast the beating stopped,
It feels like you're being told all over again,
You want to scream yourself out of your own body,
The pain is excruciating,
For a moment it feels like you're *actually* dying.

And just life that,
You're back at the beginning
Hopeless, lonely, and selfish.

NOTHING LEFT IN ME

I don't have enough of myself together,
To give you any extra pieces of me,
My energy has been leaking through my pores,
And all people seem to want is to suck it out of me,
But I have nothing left to spare,
I can hardly hold myself up,
You're sucking me completly dry,
Draining me of the energy I have left,
I'm afraid I might collapse.

DON'T GIVE UP ON ME

If I'm not evil how come I keep making you cry?
If I'm so sweet why do I still wanna die?
Keep feeding me these thoughts,
I'll chew them up and spit them at you.
I'm still just as lost,
As when you asked me 6 months ago,
Still just as broken from the last time you tried to fix me,
Tideously trying to glue me back together,
But the glue has stopped sticking,
I keep falling even more apart,
I think its time you threw me out,
Maybe its time youd just give up.

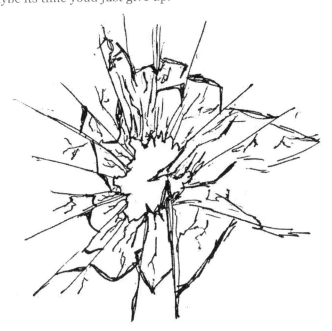

PARANOIA

My mama always told me not to trust no one,
That's why when I look into his eyes all I see is the sun,
It's bright and shiny and so beautiful,
But it's also burning through my eyes,
Which is oh, so painful,
It can kill me if I get too close,
It can kill me from a distance.
Your words are pretty,
But they're just words to me.
My mama always told me not to trust no one,
So every time I let you in,
There's a knife underneath the sofa,
You might not understand,
You might even call it paranoia.
My mama raised me to believe,
No ones out here for the good,
She told me not to trust no one,
Especially the misunderstood.

UNBALANCED

Only time I feel sane,
Mercury's retrograde,
What's wrong with my brain?
I can't feel any pain,
Numb to my lungs,
Rotting out my chest,
Cared so much,
Now I don't remember,
Remember what I was slitting my wrist over last week.

Manic behavior,
Calling for a psychological counselor.
Let me step all over you,
As I try to find my balance,
If you can love me now,
When I'm normal I can't have you around

Scaring you in the middle of the night,
Thinking I've become an exorcist,
Spasms in my bed,
As I scream at you to leave,
When all I really want is you to grab my neck,
Choke me out,
So I don't feel this pain,
I don't wanna feel a thing.

They think I'm this sweet little angel,
Little do they know what you have to handle,
And you do it well baby, you do,
That's what I'm afraid of,
How much am I hurting you?

NOW IM AFRAID

I watch the angels dance around your head all night,
they're afraid of a girl like me;
Dying inside.
Lie next to me while I lay here and cry,
I see you twitch in your sleep,
While you dream about me.
I'm in love with you baby,
It's never been more clear.
But everytime you leave,
They whisper in my ear.
They tell me I'm not good enough for you,
I'm not who you should be with,
And when I close my eyes to sleep,
I have nothing left to dream with.
Now my dreams turn to nightmares,
And I'm afraid to live without you,
I know I have attachment issues,
I realized at the age of two,
But ever since I lost him,
I can't fathom losing you.

DEEPER THAN THE OCEAN

He says I talk about death too much,
I think I know what he means,
He told me maybe it's too dark,
For my actual aching heart,
Doesn't want it too cause me anymore pain,
But I just can't seem to let it go,

Is there anywhere deeper than the ocean?
Because I swear I wanna go.

But no matter what seemed to be going on, the pain never really seemed to stop...

DIDN'T BELIEVE HE MEANT IT

I begged him "don't leave me",
He begged her "please go",
I can't do this with those watery eyes following me everywhere I
go,
I can't be anything they want me to be,
With the guilt of your pain caressing me,
He whispered he loved me,
I didn't believe he meant it.

Went on to be the star that he always wanted,
Would hear from him once a month,
Twice if I was lucky,
He'd tell me he still loves me,
Still the only one he ever wanted,
I didn't believe he meant it.

Until the day he told me just one last time,
Hours before he fell asleep,
With nothing but a pill,
and an empty stomach.

I GUESS YOU'RE REALLY GONE

I've never gone this long without you,
It's like life goes on but something's missing,
The color is still there,
They just keep on dimming.
I remember your touch,
But it's getting lighter every month.
I remember your voice,
But I can't remember the words all that much,
I can't remember if your favorite color was purple or red,
And some days I wake up without you in my head.

THOSE BROWN EYES

I'd still yank the stars out of the skies,
Just to put the twinkle back into your eyes.

THIS WON'T BE THE END

I pray I dream of you tonight,
That is my only wish;
To make some new memories with you,
Even if it's just a dream,
Even if they don't exist.

LOST HOPE

I remember thinking I'd see your face
somewhere,
I remember thinking every shadow
was you,
Even my own,
Sometimes I still do,
It's kind of calming,
To want to see the dead,
To walk into the house,
Without turning the lights on,
Hoping maybe you'll see a glimpse of
them,
Hoping maybe they won't run away,
But its become very disappointing,
When you hope,
And hope,
And hope,
And no one ever shows.

So I started to turn the lights on,
When I walked into the house,
I even started to be afraid of some
shadows,
I'd close my eyes if I saw something frightening,
And now I'm afraid that I may have missed you,
Maybe you showed up,
And I wasn't even there to greet you.

... At some point you just start to get used to it

WAKING UP

One day you wake up,
And you stop wiping the tears that fell from your nightmares,
You wake up and you come to terms with it,
You wake up and it seems normal,
Something you never thought would be,
Is now just your life,

This pain you thought would never subside,
Just becomes your daily mind.

YOU WERE BY MY SIDE ONCE, I KNOW YOU WERE

I won't tell you it's going to be
okay,
Becausec it's not,
But I will say that you'll see
the world in color again,
It might never be as bright,
But you'll adapt to the pastels,
And sometimes it may even
seem like a delight,

One day you'll be able to open your front door,
And notice things you've hadnt noticed before,
Like the birds song who lived there all along,

The small signs of life,
They won't always make you want to cry,
One day you may just cherrish,
All the time you had with them by your side.

ONE YEAR

5 am,
5am my mother told me,
Just by the look on her face,
I knew something was about to end,
And just by the sound of your name,
I thought I might be better off dead,
I screamed and I cried,
I called my best friend 42 times.

That day finally passed,
When it felt like it would never end,
I looked for you with my eyes wide open,
In every dark corner,
In every road bend.
I thought if I just saw you,
Id convince myself I've made this all up in my head.

1 week went by,
My lack of sleep screaming through my eyes,
I didn't look for you,
All I could do was deny.

Then a month had gone by,
And I could've sworn I saw you once or twice.
In my dreams you would tell me,
"It'll all be alright",
In the street I'd see shadows,
That were just about your height,
Id lay down in the dark,
And imagine your eyes.

I blinked with mine,
And 3 month had gone by,
I visited a psychic,
I would no longer believe my little mind tricks,
She told me "he's here",
He says you look a mess,
To get your shit together,
And get some better rest,
You told me you were with me,
Everywhere I go,
And when i'm driving to stop crying,
So I'd stear with more control
You could still make laugh,
In a place so unknown.

By the time 6 months hit,
Something switched,
I was just sick of hearing it,
"He's with you,
hes here,
hes in a better place dear",
I was so sick of seeing these pictures of you,
With all the same captions,
3 months to 6,
I was sick of being reminded,
I was sick of the pictures that just wouldn't move,
And sick of all the videos I looked at too soon,
Sick of waking up from sweet dreams,
To my world full of grief.

Some days are worse,
Some days are better,
9 months had gone by,
And I finally washed your dirty sweater,
But you know what?
I can still smell you on that sweater,
And my mind still plays those little tricks,
Because I've seen you in the strangest of weather,
I even hear your voice,
When I read through your old letters,
I felt your love then,
I'll feel it forever.

And if you asked me last year,
What I would do?
I would've told you I couldn't survive,
I could never.
But 1 year has gone by,
And somehow I'm still put together.
Some days are worse,
Somedays are better.

If you asked what I would do if this happened before it actually did, I would have told you I could never live in a world without him.
But somehow you do.
You wake up every day,
Even on the days you wish you didn't.
I waited for the world to stand still, but it never did.
And as selfish as it was, I wanted everyone in the world to grieve your loss with me.
But they dont,
life just goes on,
and not because you want it to, it just does.

You try your hardest not to think about the could've beens,
because those are what hurt the most.
And you even try not to think them at all sometimes.
But It just becomes something thats apart of you, engraved in you forever.
Like it's written in you dna.
Sometimes I wish it was just written on my forehead so i didn't have to explain it so much,
but I do.
Because I want too, it's just something I want to share.
A pain too heavy to hold in.
It changes you forever,
beyond anything you could ever imagine.
I am a completely different person then I was.
I am so much stronger than I ever even knew.

But no matter how strong that doesn't take the pain away,
it just makes it somewhat livable.

The human body is quite amazing that way, in its will to survive.

Now the end is always the hardest,
and I feel as though this is abrupt.

But so was his.

Made in the
USA
Middletown, DE